Big Al Tel

The Recruiting System
(Sponsoring Magic)

by
Tom Schreiter

KAAS Publishing
P.O. Box 890084
Houston, TX 77289

http://www.fortunenow.com

Phone: (281) 280-9800

Printed in the United States of America

Copyright © 1985 by KAAS Publishing

Revised 1999

ISBN 1-892366-00-2

About the author

Tom Schreiter has spent the better part of his network marketing career destroying myths and "old wives tales." So much
time and energy have been wasted on obsolete, useless, and
ill-conceived business building techniques that Tom has found
audiences eager to learn new, tested and proven methods of
building solid organizations. His motto is "No theory! Just
facts that work!"

This book is a collection of mini-lessons that has his unique,
straightforward, concise writing style. In a few words or examples Tom brings to light the real answers to network marketing leadership challenges. You'll find the same humor and
directness that has endeared Tom to his workshop audiences
throughout the United States. So sit down and prepare yourself for an exciting reading experience.

—Big Al

"Big Al"

WARNING

This book could be dangerous to your health. The results of following the enclosed directions will greatly increase your income. With increased income comes the stress and worry of how to properly invest your excess money. The authors and publishers of this book will assume no responsibility for nervous breakdowns caused by over-abundant wealth.

Just one good idea pays the price of this book. We certainly hope you will receive more than one.

This book is so valuable you shouldn't even tell the IRS you own it.

Table of Contents

Distributor "Joe"

Distributor "Joe"

Joe Distributor woke up early Saturday morning. All week long he had been looking forward to his day off to do some "real recruiting." No job to interfere today, just 100% effort to sponsor distributors. After finishing a hearty breakfast, Joe looked at the clock — 8:30 a.m.— time to make those phone appointments.

A little hesitant, Joe dials the first number. The phone rings three times and Joe quickly hangs up. "They might still be in bed, I guess I shouldn't be calling this early," Joe thinks to himself. "I should do some goal-setting for an hour."

At 9:30 a.m., Joe finishes his revised goal and projections chart showing how much bonus he will receive if each of his 10th level distributors sponsor just one person a week who average $20.30 in weekly volume. He has also calculated the number of personal speaking engagements he can fit into his schedule when he reaches superstar status.

But first, Joe has to sponsor that **first distributor.**

At 9:35 a.m., Joe makes his second phone call. The line is busy. With a feeling of relief, Joe thinks, "He probably wouldn't be interested anyway." Since Joe has failed to get an appointment with his first two prospects, he decides to research his prospect list to see who else he can contact. While researching his list, Joe takes this opportunity to divide the good prospects from the medium prospects from the lousy prospects. Now that he has them organized, he writes all their names and pertinent data on 3 x 5 cards and sets up a beautiful file system that would be the envy of IBM.

At 11:45 a.m., Joe begins to feel a little guilty that he has done everything but recruiting this morning. He thinks to himself, "I'm not really afraid to talk to people or get rejects, I'm just setting a good foundation for a big afternoon. As a matter of fact, I'm ready to go out now and recruit in a big way."

As Joe gets ready to leave the house, he suddenly comes to his senses and remarks, "Whoops, it is almost lunch time, I'd better eat before I leave."

At 1:00 p.m., Joe finally leaves his house and pulls out of the driveway. But where should he go first? No appointments. No plans.

Joe gets up his courage and heads for the little neighborhood shopping district to make some cold calls. His opportunity is good and these are small business people he is going to call on . . . should be a perfect match for success.

Mr. Shoemaker had a line of customers in his shop, so Joe wisely passed him by. Mr. Tile and Carpet had only one person looking around, but if Joe would be rejected, that customer might think poorly of Joe and his opportunity. Mrs. Florist had a sour face, best not stop in and make her more upset. At the shoe store, only a young salesperson was on the floor. However, if Joe were to present his opportunity to him, he might be caught by the manager of the store and thrown out. Ah, but Mr. Watch Repair was alone.

Joe introduced himself. Mr. Watch Repair immediately took control by asking, "How much money is this going to cost me? How long have you been doing this? What are your credentials? Can you show me your last 12 bonus checks?"

Totally intimidated, Joe saved face by saying he was very busy and had another appointment, then he quickly left.

At 2:20 p.m. Joe entered his car quite discouraged. He realized his self-confidence was at zero, but he wanted to make one more effort. Joe decided to drive by his friend's house and make at least one presentation.

At 2:45, Joe drove down the street in front of his friend's house, careful not to enter the driveway. From the street, Joe could see no activity through the front window. Since it appeared no one was home, Joe said to himself, "Well, now is probably a good time to head home and take inventory. A successful businessman must have proper record-keeping to succeed."

"Big Al" . . .
A Clue To Success

Joe Distributor had a professional recruiter for a sponsor named *Big Al*. When Big Al called Joe to see how Saturday went, he already knew what Joe would report.

He said, "Joe, I know you were eager to do well, and I know that insecure feeling that creeps over all of us when we recruit. I think after that experience you may be willing to listen to my advice on how to cure that problem permanently."

Joe's spirits immediately lifted as he hurried to Big Al's house to learn the secret solution to his recruiting problem.

When Joe arrived, Big Al said, "One lesson is worth 10,000 words. Most distributors get good advice but never realize the value or put it to use. I am not going to tell you the magic solution to your recruiting problem. You'll learn that for yourself. What I'd like you to do now is make a few phone calls and set some recruiting appointments for Tuesday night. Don't worry about who you set the appointments with, since I'll go with you and I will do all the talking. You'll just tag along and watch, okay? Just say to your friends, 'Are you interested in some extra money? I want you to meet this guy, Big Al. Let's get together at your house Tuesday night for 20 minutes. You'll just love to meet this guy.'"

Joe felt this was not too hard. After all, he didn't have to do anything but set an appointment. The whole presentation would be done by Big Al. Joe could just sit back, let his friends blast away with all kinds of questions and objections, and watch Big Al handle them and make them distributors.

Big Al pointed to the telephone and said, "Why not make a call or two now?"

Joe was motivated. In just 20 minutes he had set up four appointments for Tuesday night. And handling questions on the phone was a breeze since Joe's attitude was super-positive.

When asked, "What's it all about?" Joe would reply, "I just want you to meet Big Al, he's got a lot of ideas on making money and you'll think he's a pretty neat guy."

Big Al turned to Joe and said, "Go home and relax. We'll meet at your house on Tuesday night at 5:30. You have already accomplished more in 20 minutes than most distributors do in a week."

Two Against One:
The Unfair Advantage

Tuesday night went so smoothly that Joe was at a loss for words. One appointment wasn't interested, one appointment had to think it over, and **two appointments became distributors.** Imagine two new first level distributors in one evening!

And it was easy. Joe just introduced Big Al to his prospect and Big Al calmly showed the opportunity. When Big Al was done, the prospect either joined or not. There was no magical presentation, no high pressure, just a simple explanation that Joe could probably do just as well.

But what was amazing is how the prospects reacted. They listened to every word Big Al said. They treated him with respect. There were no cynical objections. The prospects were on their best behavior. That made Big Al's job easy.

When Big Al and Joe arrived at Joe's house later that evening, Joe asked Big Al in to explain the wonderful happenings of that evening. Big Al smiled and told Joe to begin taking notes.

Big Al said, "The secret of recruiting this evening was simple. **There were two of us and only one of them.** They were at an unfair advantage. All we had to do was convince one person to our way of thinking. And our thinking must have some merit, because there are two of us already who share it. It is a lot easier for the prospect to join our enthusiasm than it is for him to convince two of us that we're wrong. Besides, he wants to think like we do. He wants extra money, too."

"This may seem simple but all professional recruiters work in pairs. Knowing this is vital to your success, let's take a closer look at **why** professionals work in pairs:

1. When you visit a friend he may side-track you with stories, sports talk, and chatter about your families. He can joke with you, tease you, and give you all kinds of grief just for the fun of it.

   But the scene changes drastically when you are with a stranger. He is polite since he doesn't know me. He feels I'm an expert because I'm a stranger. I may be your boss, so he is on his best behavior not to embarrass you. He may feel he can intimidate you, but with a stranger along, he will be cooperative and business-like.

2. Your prospect sees only you, not the company you represent. If he feels you are in some way inadequate personally, he will reject the opportunity based on you, not the company. However, if a stranger is along whom he doesn't know personally, he must make a decision on the facts at hand, not on you and your present position.

3. When two people work as a team, their self-confidence is at a high level. They keep each other motivated. It's not like taking on the world alone. If you are by yourself, you are probably afraid of rejection, afraid to make appointments, and more likely to avoid contact with prospects. That's why you spent Saturday doing paperwork. If you had a companion, each would work hard not to let

the other one down. If each were to make four appointments, you'd be sure to keep up your end of the load. Neither person wants to be the first one to quit.

4. When two distributors make a presentation, one talks, the other keeps quiet and observes. The observer does not have to worry about making sure the presentation has all the information in order, etc., so he is free to closely observe the prospect and listen for clues to his motivation. When it comes time for the prospect to make a decision, the observer may be able to help with some vital information that otherwise might be overlooked.

5. Two distributors working together accomplish more than each working separately. I'm sure you now see why you are much more efficient working as a team. Professionals look for efficiency.

6. **If you do not work as a team and have your new distributors recruit alone, you are then assuming the following:**

(a) Your new distributors have instant and total knowledge of your business.

(b) Your new distributors are blessed with unlimited self-confidence and can handle rejection alone.

     (c) Your new distributors became instantly competent in presenting the opportunity by virtue of filling out their distributor applications.

To assume the above would be ludicrous. Therefore, the only alternative is to work as a team.

7. When two work together, there is an opportunity to evaluate each presentation. They can review the good points and the not-so-good aspects of that particular presentation to make their next one even better. Having two separate viewpoints, the presenter and the observer, is invaluable.

"As you can see, Joe, there is a lot of logic that dictates that recruiting should be done in pairs. For the next two weeks, you and I will work together Tuesday nights and Saturdays. We'll need four appointments each Tuesday and six appointments on Saturdays. That's ten a week. I'll make five appointments and you make five. Fair enough?"

Joe enthusiastically agreed. This was going to be easy. All his fears about recruiting were gone and Joe saw a bright future with lots of distributors.

The Payoff

After two weeks Joe had 15 distributors in his group. It was almost becoming routine. On Tuesday evenings and Saturdays, Big Al and Joe would present the opportunity and let the prospects decide if they wanted to join. No magic, no high pressure. Just show the opportunity.

Big Al and Joe were having coffee when Big Al announced, "Joe, your training is done. You're on your own now. You've heard my presentation so many times, you can say it better than me."

Joe looked bewildered, "But we are a team, aren't we?"

Big Al laughed and said, "Joe, I don't want you to go out and recruit alone, I want you to team up with your new distributors. Sure, you and I can eventually sponsor 1,000 distributors ourselves, but that's not how network marketing works. You've got to work smart – not hard.

"You have to train your distributors just like I trained you. Wouldn't you rather have five or ten of your new distributors out recruiting, instead of you doing it all? Don't you think your new distributors will get discouraged unless you work with them as a team? Besides, Joe, you are going to run out of friends to talk to.

"Instead of making cold calls, running ads, etc., doesn't it make more sense to be talking to friends? You have 15 new distributors, some motivated, some not. Ask them to set appointments just like I asked you. You'll probably have five to eight distributors who are serious about the opportunity and will want you to work with them. Working with those five to eight serious distributors will keep you busy for a long, long time.

"You'll then have a large, strong, and deep organization of distributors. This is the fastest and surest way of becoming a superstar in network marketing."

Joe did some quick mental calculations. If he could work with just five of his new distributors so they would each have 15 distributors that would be 75 new distributors in his group! Plus, he would now have five distributors fully trained that could work with their distributors. That could be hundreds more distributors in his group. Joe was beginning to understand the word "efficiency."

Instead of each distributor floundering about on his own, by using teamwork, Joe could have hundreds of distributors in his organization in just two or three months. Big Al spent three weeks training Joe, so it would only take Joe two or three months to train his five or eight key distributors by working with them two at a time. Joe could work with one distributor on Tuesdays and Saturdays and a different distributor on Wednesdays and Thursdays.

Just think, in 60 to 90 days, Joe would have a group that would be the envy of his peers. All Joe had to do was follow The System.

Big Al pointed out to Joe that he could become a superstar just by using the basics he learned in the last three weeks. However, Big Al insisted that he and Joe meet weekly to keep Joe on course and to improve Joe's recruiting skills.

Joe then thanked Big Al for all the help, not realizing that Big Al had just added another strong downline group of distributors through Joe.

Not Everyone Is
A Worker

Two weeks later while having coffee, Joe told Big Al the wisdom of The System. Joe realized that to sponsor too many new first level distributors would be senseless. As a person would be working with his brand new recruits, he would be losing his original recruits by lack of attention.

It makes sense to limit the number of first level distributors. But what if only two or three of the original 15 distributors were serious workers? What should be done with the other nine or ten unmotivated distributors? Did we make a mistake in sponsoring obvious unmotivated distributors?

Big Al answered, "It is well known that unmotivated distributors use the product and can be good wholesale customers. You may have hundreds of dollars of volume monthly just servicing your unmotivated distributors. Certainly we should help them and not ignore them.

"Unmotivated distributors have different goals than you, Joe. They may have joined only to sell and make a few extra dollars, or just wanted to buy wholesale for themselves. My personal organization does several thousand dollars monthly of 'internal consumption.'

"The problem here, Joe, is that you are missing the big picture. You did not sponsor an unmotivated distributor, you sponsored **a valuable contact who knows dozens of good quality prospects, who when sponsored, will become workers.** In other words, don't judge the unmotivated distributor for what he might do. Judge him for the potential distributors in his organization.

"Your job is to work in depth, get referrals, and work to replace your unmotivated distributor. Surely he knows at least one person who can become a good worker in your organization.

"The professional recruiters readily admit that they probably didn't sponsor most of their workers. Their workers were probably second level, third level, or even 10th level distributors who like cream, rose to the top.

"Never hesitate to sponsor an unmotivated distributor. His personal goals may change and he could develop into a worker, or he may lead you to a worker you would have never met."

Myth Killing

The following week while at coffee, Joe confessed to being tempted to do some exciting innovations in recruiting. Joe had researched some good ideas and wanted to know if he could implement these for faster growth.

Not that The System wasn't working, as a matter of fact, Joe now had over 85 distributors in his organization after only seven weeks in the business. It was that these new ideas sounded so fabulous, that Joe just couldn't wait to try them out.

Big Al smiled and took a deep breath. "Joe, I guess it's time to do some myth-killing. Every distributor has his own pet idea on how to recruit fast. Some may work partially, some may only collect applications, and some only work in unusual circumstances. The reason pros use The System is it works. Anyone can use it and leap to the top in a matter of weeks.

"The reason I insisted on meeting weekly was to keep you on track, Joe. Following various recruiting ideas in a scattered manner will only bog you down. Keep on The System and avoid being swayed from your present course. But I don't want you to take my word on it. Let's examine together some of the major recruiting myths and analyze their weaknesses. With this knowledge, we won't be tempted to stray from our proven course."

The next three hours were spent analyzing why many of the other recruiting methods do not work consistently for most beginning distributors. Here are some of the major myths and their weaknesses:

1. **Newspaper Ads — Help Wanted.** Imagine an unemployed 17-year-old reading the paper. No money, no car, just looking for a few dollars for his next date. The problem with Help Wanted Ads is that you reach the unemployed who need money now. They can't wait several months to build a business. They want to know how

much salary the job pays. The real people you want are those with jobs who want to build a part-time business. Since they don't read the Help Wanted Ads, why advertise there?

2. **Newspaper Ads — Business Opportunity.** While the readership is small, you do reach business people looking to buy a business. They probably have accumulated enough cash to hire a manager to run their network marketing business for them. But is network marketing a business you can buy? No, it is a business that requires personal effort. Obviously this is not the best place to find workers willing to go out and start a business.

3. **Unemployment Office.** The majority of the people at the office fall into two categories: (1) those who do not wish to look for a job and just want to collect unemployment (we certainly wouldn't want to upset these people by giving them an opportunity to work), and (2) those looking for work who have been unable to find a job. These people need a job now, not a business opportunity that will pay off in the months ahead. (See No. 1)

4. **Employment Agencies** — See No. 1.

5. **Door-to-Door.** Certainly okay for people with masochistic tendencies, but not for most normal people. Besides, it's a good way to get shot or mugged. You can't afford to lose good workers to a mugger.

6. **Direct Mail.** Wouldn't it be nice if we just
    sent out a letter and people joined? But
    what do we do with most of our junk
    mail? However, writing letters is a good
    way to pass the time and practice our
    spelling and handwriting. Also, it helps
    support the U.S. Postal Service. But as a
    recruiting tool, let us leave it for the pro-
    fessional, experienced mail order people.

7. **Telephone Soliciting.** It is 2 p.m., Thurs-
    day afternoon. You have just managed to
    put your six-month old baby to sleep. You
    are watching your favorite soap opera and
    they are about to announce the secret
    identity of the villain. The phone rings.
    What do you think your attitude would be

when a stranger says he has randomly called you to be a distributor? People are so used to telephone solicitors trying to sell them something, they just refuse to listen to any stranger's sales pitch. There surely must be an easier way.

8. **Handouts and Flyers.** Almost every distributor in network marketing feels he has written the perfect advertisement that will force the prospect to call and beg to be a distributor. He pastes them up, hands them out on corners, and slips them under doors. While it may produce some activity of unqualified prospects, its real benefit is that the distributor gets a lot of fresh air and exercise. What do we normally do when people hand us flyers and junk mail? Is this the most efficient way of reaching qualified prospects? If there were such a thing as the perfect network marketing advertisement, wouldn't everybody be recruited already?

9. **Grocery Store Bulletin Boards.** Just how many serious workers do you think read grocery store bulletin boards to find that **solid business opportunity?**

10. **Fund Raising.** Once the funds have been raised, you are left with zero distributors. Is this a way to build a solid organization? It is hard to convince an organization to use your product and hard to train them to sell it. Why put forth the effort for a one-time short-term benefit?

Big Al continued, "Surely there is some merit in each of these methods. If you have extra time, there is nothing wrong in doing them. But **do not deviate from The System.** Just because one person may have had success with one of these does not mean that you will encounter the same set of circumstances.

"Let me give you an example. At a convention, a young 17-year-old girl told of selling over $1,000 of product and sponsored several distributors by going door-to-door in her neighborhood in just one week. Everyone was excited that this young girl had shared with them the way to success.

"Needless to say, the other distributors failed. What the young girl failed to mention was that her mother was mayor of the small town, owned most of the property, and her tenants felt obligated to help her daughter.

"Another example: a young man confidently tells you about his success in helping a church raise funds through the sale of his products. What isn't mentioned is that his brother was the minister who ordered the members to sell this product.

In other words, get all the facts. Most times there are special circumstances behind these inefficient methods of prospecting. Don't follow them blindly. **Use The System and let the amateur recruiters chase their tails trying to make these other methods work.**"

The Traveling Salesman

The following week over coffee, Joe related an interesting situation. It seems that one of Joe's most promising distributors had a hot prospect 90 miles out of town. Since it took all evening driving there and back, there was no time for other appointments. Even though the prospect wanted time to think it over, Joe was confident that he would join. Was it worth the time and effort to go out of town? Could the time be spent better making three or four presentations locally?

Big Al pulled out a blank piece of paper and began figuring. "Let's see now, 180 miles round trip at a cost of 30 cents a miles equals $54.00. You'll need a second trip to complete signing him up so that's another $54.00 for a total of $108.00. Joe, for that same $108.00 you could have bribed your next door neighbor to become a distributor and been home by 6:30 p.m.

"Plus, look at the income you lost by losing two evenings of sponsoring. How much money could you have made from those potential recruits you did not see because you were out-of-town? Total that figure with $108.00 and ask yourself if that out-of-town prospect was worth it.

"But that's not the whole story. How much time will you or your distributor lose by driving out-of-town to train this prospect? I personally sponsor people in my own backyard. You've hear the saying, **'The grass looks greener on the other side of the fence.'**

"Why not let amateur recruiters drive past 100,000 potential prospects on their way to see their out-of-town hot prospect? There will be plenty of these amateurs in your organization who do not wish to follow The System. Give them the leads and let them do the driving. As a professional recruiter, you have more important activities to occupy your time than driving."

Test Question: Distributor A, who lives in the city of Alpha, drives 100 miles to the city of Bimbo to recruit a new distributor. At the same time, Distributor B, who lives in Bimbo, drives 100 miles to the city of Alpha to recruit a new distributor.

Q. Who wins?

A. Exxon gasoline stations.

One Story Is Worth 10,000 Facts

Big Al was sharpening Joe's presentation skills. "Don't just throw out facts, tell a story. Your prospects and distributors **will remember the story long after the fact has been forgotten.** And stories are more powerful and more motivating. Don't you want to motivate your prospect or distributor? I bet you can remember an interesting story told to you by your first grade teacher. But you have probably forgotten 90% of the facts you had to memorize in high school. Proof enough?"

Big Al then shared some stories that were guaranteed to bring life to a presentation.

"Work Smart - Not Hard"

If a president of a large conglomerate earns $1,000,000 a year and a common laborer earns $10,000 a year, does this mean the president worked 100 times harder? Did the president put in 100 times more hours in a week? I doubt if the president of any conglomerate could work a 400-hour week. Why is it then that some men earn much more than others?

They work smart — not hard.

These men have found ways to provide more service, be more efficient . . . ways to lead others to more productivity. In other words, to produce more value in the same allotted time.

Who would you pay more? A man who sells $100 worth of your goods or a man who sells $1,000 worth of your goods? Obviously, you would pay the second man 10 times more. If we wish to receive more income, we must produce more service. We must find ways of working smarter — not harder.

If I needed a ditch excavated one mile long, and was willing to pay $10,000, you could apply for the job. You would take your trusty shovel and begin digging. At the end of one year the ditch would be completed. For that one mile ditch I would then pay you $10,000 because you have performed $10,000 worth of service.

On the other hand, a friend of yours could apply for the job. Your friend then rents a ditch-digging machine for $100 and finishes the ditch in one day. Has he also provided $10,000 worth of service?

Who worked smart and who worked hard?

The above story has several applications. You may tell this story to a prospect to impress on them that working for someone else is working hard, and having your own part-time business is working smart.

You may use the story with a new distributor who spends all his time looking for new first level distributors. That's working hard. Instead of trying to sponsor everyone personally, your new distributor should use The System where he may only sponsor a few personally, but end up with hundreds in his organization. That's working smart.

"Proper Education"

Let's look at how many years of our lives we spend in school:

Grade School	8 years
High School	4 years
College	4 years
	16 years

College can cost about $10,000 per year. Why do we go to college? To become successful. But in college we take English, Accounting, Business, Engineering, etc., all courses designed to make us good employees for someone else. We don't take a single course in our true "Major" . . . **Success**.

We spend 16 years of our lives and $40,000 (four years in college) and don't take even one course in how to become a **Success**. Don't you think it would be worthwhile to spend $100 and two days to attend a course and learn how to become a **Success**?

The above story is useful in motivating a distributor to attend further self-improvement training. It also can be tailored to new prospects. (Mr. Prospect, you've spent 16 years and $40,000 to learn how to be a good employee. Won't you invest $100 and two months to see if you can be as successful as your own boss?)

"Here's Your Chance"

Who makes more money? The person who owns the company or the employee who works for him? The owner, of course.

Mr. Prospect, you now have the opportunity to own your own business and decide how much money you can earn. Do you want to remain an employee and let your boss decide your earnings, or do you wish to start your own business by becoming a distributor now?

The above story helps the Prospect to make up his mind now. No need to think it over as the choice is clear; there is no middle ground.

"The Office Manager"

A young mother decides to get a full-time job to pay the many bills in raising a family. There are many sacrifices she must make:

1. She will be away from the house 8-10 hours a day. Housework and meals will suffer.

2. The children will no longer have the advantage of a full-time mother at home.

3. She will miss the wonderful experience of helping the children develop.

4. There will be less quality time with her family as evenings are spent to catch up on household duties.

But in return for these sacrifices she finds a job paying $2,000 a month. After deductions, what does she really earn?

$2,000 Salary
-350 Federal Income Tax
- 50 State Income Tax
-120 Social Security
-270 Monthly Payment on second car
- 60 Monthly Insurance payment on second car
- 50 Monthly Maintenance on second car
-130 Gasoline to and from work
-320 Babysitter
- 60 Beauty Salon
-100 Increased wardrobe needs
- 80 Insurance deductions and office gifts
-100 Meals
$ 310 Remaining to pay bills

That's earning less than $2 an hour. Is it worth 22 days a month away from the children and 176 hours of work not counting travel time? Wouldn't the young mother rather stay home if possible?

With our opportunity you can easily earn $310.00 from your home in just a few hours per week. Not only is it easier, more profitable, and fun, but you can now enjoy time with your family, too!

The above story helps people appreciate time with their families.

The Oyster Story

Suppose that you are now a professional pearl diver sitting on the dock by the sea. Every hour I give you a bucket of 100 oysters. Among the 100 oysters are five that have pearls. The other 95 are empty.

As a professional you take out the first oyster, cut it open, and find it empty. You then carefully put it back together, hold it between your hands to keep it warm, and then sit there for days hoping it will grow a pearl. Is this what you'd do?

Of course not. You would throw the empty oyster away and reach for another and another until you found one with a pearl.

However, most distributors treat their friends and alleged "good prospects" like the empty oyster. Instead of going on to a good prospect, they keep hoping, asking, inviting, and pleading with the same people week after week. They will invite the same person 17 times to an opportunity meeting! They never catch a hint. They work too long with "empty oysters."

The secret to recruiting is not in convincing people, but in sorting people. You can wear yourself out and become discouraged working with the same "empty oysters." Your job as a professional recruiter is only to sort through the prospects until you find one who wants to be a distributor. It is ten times easier to locate a prospect who wants to work, than to convince an unwilling disinterested prospect to work.

The Eagle and The Oyster

Once there were two eggs discussing what they wanted to be when they hatch. The first egg said, "I want to be an oyster when I hatch. An oyster just sits in the water. It has no decisions to make. The currents of the ocean move it about, so it doesn't have to plan. The ocean water that passes by is its food. Whatever the ocean provides is what the oyster may receive, no more, no less. That's the life for me. It may be limited, but there are no decisions, no responsibilities, just a plain existence controlled by the ocean."

The second egg said, "That's not the life for me. I wish to be an eagle. An eagle is free to go where he wants and do as he pleases. Sure he is responsible for hunting his own food and making survival decisions, but he is free to fly as high as the mountains. The eagle is in control, not controlled by others. I wish no limits placed on me. I do not wish to be a slave of the ocean. For this I am willing to pay the effort required to live the life of an eagle."

Which would you rather be an eagle or an oyster?

The above story is effective with prospects and distributors in a rut, who are complacent and just existing. It is designed to make them unhappy with the crumbs others throw their way, and to motivate them to make their own destinies.

"The Best Investment"

"Do you smoke? If you smoke cigarettes, a pack a day will cost you $20 a week. Do you drink coffee? Two cups a day will cost you about $20.00 a week. Yet how many distributors did those cigarettes and coffee get you?

"None!

"Why not invest $12.95 for this book and start getting yourself a bunch of distributors? As a businessman, wouldn't you be willing to spend less than the cost of coffee for a guaranteed system for success?" (Thinly disguised biased commercial.)

Wouldn't you want each of your distributors using The System?

The Two
Magic Questions

Joe Distributor said, "Those stories are just great, but sometimes I have trouble getting started. I need something to break the ice. I've tried talking about the weather and sports, but that's a waste of time and the prospect knows it. Besides, I'm uncomfortable saying, 'The weather sure is nice, how about looking at this business opportunity?' That doesn't flow at all. Plus, if there were some way to break the ice and qualify the prospect at the same time, I could save lots of time by only talking to interested, qualified people. I seem to be making a lot of presentations to people who are totally uninterested. Do you have a solution?"

Big Al always had the answers. He was a pro. He used The System.

Big Al replied, "You can **save a lot of time by prequalifying your prospects.** At the same time you can also 'break the ice' and get down to business. But first let us take a look at what qualities a prospect must have to be a distributor."

"Intelligence? No, you and I have both sponsored some dummies. A good salesman? No, we know some successful distributors who were both shy and unassuming. A positive attitude? Not a chance. There are plenty of negative distributors in the world. There are really two very important qualities the prospect should have to become a good distributor.

1. "Desire. The prospect must desire to earn some extra money. However, the biggest mistake amateur recruiters make is confusing **need** with **desire**. They are totally different. People who need extra money many times have no desire to earn it. The amateur recruiter concentrates on all the unemployed and 'broke' people who do not wish to put forth an extra effort to get ahead. This could also include people with 'dead end' jobs who only wish to watch TV in the evening. An unemployed person may need extra money, but may not have the desire to go out and earn it. He may be satisfied just where he is. The amateurs spend endless hours trying to reprogram needy people who do not have desire. Playing psychologist may be good for the ego but bad for the pocketbook."

2. "Time. Everyone has 24 hours in a day. What we are looking for is someone who is willing to set aside time to work your business opportunity. You may find people with nothing to do who insist they just can't set aside the time. TV, bowling, etc., are just too important to

44

give up. These prospects are not for us. We want prospects who can commit to six or ten hours a week for their business. If someone really busy says he can only set aside four hours a week, that's okay too. At least he made a commitment. Besides, busy people get things done."

"Now that we know the qualities required of a good distributor, it's easy to find out if they qualify. All we have to do is ask. For example:

Q. Do you want to earn some extra money?

Q. Are you willing to set aside six to ten hours per week?

"We just **listen** to their answers to determine if they qualify. Just that simple. With these two magic questions we also 'break the ice' and are immediately down to business.

"The magic really isn't in the questions. The magic is in the answers. Pay close attention to what your prospect says and how he says it."

Joe Distributor took careful note to use the two magic questions on his very next appointment. With this new information Joe felt he was getting close to becoming a recruiting pro.

*"Give the person
with a need . . . a job.*

*Give the person
with a desire . . . an opportunity!"*

— Big Al

The Big Payoff

Big Al spent one entire evening showing Joe Distributor the "Big Picture." The really big distributor organizations are not one superstar who personally recruited 1,000, but one professional r ecruiter who sponsored a few good distributors and helped each of them get 100-200 distributors down their organization.

Wouldn't a person feel better having five to ten self-sufficient, well-trained "Generals" with properly trained organizations, than to have 1,000 untrained, unmotivated "Privates" with no organization?

Here is how we get those deep, secure, profitable organizations.

1. We work as a team with our first level distributor (who is a worker, not an unmotivated distributor) until we have built at least 15 distributors in his group.

2. We help our first level distributor identify five to eight good workers he can work with as a team.

3. Because our first level distributor may not be able to work with each of his own workers immediately, we help by teaming with some of his workers. Even though we are now teaming with our second or third level distributors, we are still building our organization by training and recruiting more downline distributors.

4. The System will give us the following distributors per worker:

   1 worker

   6 sub workers

   9 unmotivated distributors/product users.

If we have six or seven good workers, we will develop hundreds of distributors in our organization as they duplicate our success.

5. We make sure each worker in our organization has his own personal copy of this book. Don't give this book to an unmotivated distributor, as he may be offended that we asked him to work. We then review The System with our workers on a regular basis to help keep them on track.

6. Only after our present protégé's organization is fully trained do we add another protégé. We don't spread ourselves too thin, and we must finish what we started.

Big Al asked if there were any questions.

Joe replied, "None at all, Big Al. My group is over 300 already and I'm not deviating one step from The System. I always make presentations with someone else. And with information I've received, I'm beginning to become a recruiting pro just like you."

How To Get Your Spouse To Believe In Goal-Setting

A problem in network marketing is the difference in commitment among spouses. Many times one spouse is totally sold on attending meetings, trainings, and rallies, while the other spouse complains about no quality time with the family and too much time spent away from home.

This is a perfect formula for friction, discontent, and divorce. One spouse sees the network marketing opportunity as a way to achieve some specific financial goals. The other spouse does not believe that network marketing can be the vehicle to attain goals. The unbelieving spouses want certain financial goals, but their confidence in their spouses and network marketing is zero. How do we solve this problem? The following story should give a clue:

Billy Believer was an excited distributor for Acme Corporation. Although he had just started, he was beginning to show a small amount of success. The reason? Billy had just attended a company training seminar where he had learned to focus his efforts and to set one goal at a time.

Billy's goal was a brand new Cadillac. Billy would eat, sleep, and talk about his new Cadillac and when he was going to get it. To help visualize his goal, Billy cut out pictures of Cadillacs and pasted them in every room in his house. He pasted the largest one right in the middle of the bathroom mirror so that every morning he would be reminded of his goal.

Unfortunately, Mrs. Billy Believer did not share Billy's devotion to goal sharing. She hated all the pictures around the house, the constant conversations about Cadillacs, and Billy's blind belief that visualizing goals can help them come true. But the thing she hated most was the big Cadillac picture in the middle of her bathroom mirror. Every morning when Billy left, she would take down the picture. Every evening before Billy would go to bed, he would repaste the picture of his favorite Cadillac on the bathroom mirror.

This pasting and re-pasting went on for six months. Then something happened. Billy had saved enough money from his network marketing program for a down payment for the Cadillac.

That evening Billy confidently drove home in the brand new Cadillac, honked the horn when he arrived, and sat in glory as his spouse looked out the window in amazement.

The next morning there was a picture of a mink coat pasted on the bathroom mirror.

Close Before You Start

Prospects and salesmen have a psychological war during the entire sales presentation. The salesman gives reason after reason why he should buy. If the prospect doesn't arm himself with faults about the product, he will have no defense when the salesman closes. Therefore, the prospect must concentrate on finding reasons not to buy, avoid trap commitments laid by the salesman, and be on guard against any sales tricks that the salesman may use to get him.

With all these problems the prospect does not have the time to really listen or weigh the good points why he should buy. No wonder salesmen have such a hard time communicating with their prospects.

The solution to this universal sales problem is simple. Merely put the prospect at ease by telling him:

1. Most people buy your product.

2. The total cost of your product.

3. "Reasons" why he shouldn't buy.

4. That you will just present the facts and then it's up to him.

The secret is to tell the prospect these four things **BEFORE** you make your sales presentation.

Here are two examples of the above technique:

(a)   Mr. Prospect, most people I talk with join Acme Network marketing because they see how this can really help their incomes. After all, the total cost of getting started in our program is only $49.00; that's less than the cost of a good newspaper ad. As a matter of fact, the only two reasons people don't join are: they don't really understand our program; or that times are so tough, they just can't afford $49.00 right away. What I'm going to do is just present to you the basic facts about our opportunity and if you like it, fine, we'll get started. If you don't, fine, that's okay too. Fair enough?

(b)   Mr. Prospect, most people just love our fabulous Acme Widget. They're always telling their friends about it. After all, it only costs $30.00 and that works out to only $1.00 a day, less than cigarettes if you think about it. You know, the only reasons people don't buy the fabulous Acme Widget is that they just can't believe how well it works, or their budget just can't set the $30.00 aside. Anyway, let me show you how it works and if you like it, fine, buy one and surprise your wife. If you don't like it, that's okay too. Fair enough?

By using this simple four-step technique **BEFORE** your sales presentation, your closing ratio will increase dramatically. Here is why this technique works wonders with your prospect:

1. You have told your prospect that most people buy your product or opportunity. Your prospect does not want to be the first one to try it. He wants to know if others have made the decision to buy. Since most people buy your product, the prospect's natural tendency is to want to join the majority.

2. You have told your prospect the total cost of your product unlike most "salesmen" he has encountered. They usually hide the price and spring it out at the very end of their presentation. The prospect worries throughout the entire presentation when the price will be surprised on him and how much it will be. By revealing the price first, his mind is now clear to listen to your product's features and benefits.

3. You build trust and confidence in your prospect by telling him the entire cost in the beginning. He looks upon you as an honest businessman, not as a salesman that holds back information and tries to trick him. Even if your price is "high" or "shocking," he will want to hear about your product to see why it is so good to command such a price.

4. This technique gives you a more "unbiased, low-pressure, I don't care" approach versus the "high-pressure, you have to buy it" approach. The prospect's defenses will go down when he sees that you are not attacking his jugular vein.

When handled properly, this low-key approach motivates your prospect to want to qualify for your product. He starts selling himself.

5. By giving your prospect "reasons" not to buy, you have taken the pressure off. He doesn't have to fight you why he should not buy, because he knows you'll accept those reasons. By removing this fear, your prospect can now listen and concentrate on the features and benefits of your presentation.

6. If you plan properly, the "reasons" not to buy really force the prospect to buy. In the above two examples we have subtly said to the prospect, "Everyone buys unless he doesn't understand or is too poor." This also helps you isolate objections at the end of your presentation. Your prospect either needs more information or he just doesn't have the money.

7. By telling your prospect that it's okay if he buys or not, you again are relieving the sales pressure he naturally places on himself. However, by his agreeing to "Fair enough?" he is committing himself to a decision NOW. This helps prevent the "I'll think it over" objection when used properly.

How To Kill A Group

Norman Negative had a problem. His group volume was not growing according to his expectations. Since any problem for Norman could not possibly be his fault, he took the time to investigate and search for a reason for his group's lack of production. After careful analysis, the culprit was located. Norman's network marketing company had a lousy home office that just didn't support his group's efforts with contests and customer service. Why, the fact that his company was "killing" his group just infuriated Norman beyond control.

Of course, nothing could have been further from the truth. The rest of the company's distributors were growing at a fantastic rate. Norman probably compared his group's progress with the other leaders and felt quite inadequate. Rather than blame his own leadership, he looked outside for an excuse for his group's failure. If Norman's actions had stopped at blaming the home office, the damage to his group would have been minimal. However, Norman, like most negative leaders, continued on to prove his point. His week's itinerary went something like this.

Sunday

Complain to the family why the world is against him. No matter how hard he tried, circumstances outside his control continued to force him into failure. He predicted that by the end of the week his group would be totally discouraged with his network marketing company. Little did he realize that he was going to produce a self-fulfilling prophecy.

Monday

Norman took his normal prospecting time to sit and write a letter to the home office. He enumerated the problems they were causing for his group and told them they needed competent people like himself to run the company. Of course, he offered no positive solutions, but he did manage to get several insults included toward his regional home office area representative.

Later on Monday evening, Norman attended the weekly training meeting with a long face and a satirical attitude. The other leaders attempted to stay away from him, as they were busy helping their new distributors set goals. Norman was still able to corner his sponsor and dump all his problems on her. He also mentioned that she was stupid for participating with a company that would do all those terrible things to his group. His sponsor was able to take Norman away to the coffee shop for a private conversation before he contaminated the rest of the group. Not receiving a sympathetic audience, Norman went home more furious than ever. More drastic steps must be taken to avenge this terrible wrong.

Tuesday

Norman personally called his inactive distributors and asked for all the reasons for their inactivity. If they didn't have reasons, Norman was glad to provide them with several. Norman took painstaking notes on all that was perceived wrong with the company and added his own embellishments. Norman knew that if their sponsors who were still active would be aware of all this vital information surely they too would make the intelligent decision to complain and be upset also.

Tuesday night Norman called his active distributors and dumped all his problems on them. And because his upline and the home office were unresponsive to him, Norman felt that a meeting for his entire group to get together and complain was imperative. The meeting was set for Thursday night.

Wednesday

Norman called the home office and asked why they hadn't responded to his letter yet. He informed them that their attitude to the field was a disgrace and questioned their morals, ethics, and intelligence. He made a point of ruining his relationship with his regional home office representative. His representative hung up the phone and thought to himself that the only future communication with this negative complainer was going to be one way; he would have to call. Life was too short for him to initiate verbal abuse by calling Norman.

Wednesday night was spent calling his upline sponsors to see if they would attend Thursday night's complaint session. Norman emphasized that all of them getting together to complain would be helpful. Most of his upline sponsors begged off as they had recruiting and retailing appointments.

Thursday

That evening, all of Norman's distributors arrived with long faces. Over the past two days they had evaluated their progress in their company and came to the conclusion that their lack of success just had to be caused by factors other than themselves. No way could they personally be responsible for their results. With Norman's leadership the meeting concluded with the consensus, "That the world wasn't being fair to their group." The only course of action was to quit making efforts to correct the situation and to jointly hold "misery loves company" meetings on a weekly basis. After all, they would all need to have some activity to fill the void left by their future non-activity with their company.

Friday

Norman began early in the morning to make a calendar of the future meetings of the "Whiners & Complainers Club." On the agenda of each meeting would be a discussion on how to increase membership. If they were destined not to make any more money in network marketing, then it must be their duty to spread their afflictions on any positive, working, motivated distributor they could find.

Saturday

Norman Negative spends the day trying to rebalance the family's tight budget. Without the extra income from his network marketing company, the family would have to make several sacrifices to live within their means. And Norman thought to himself, "It's so unfair, the way the world is treating me, my network marketing group, and my family."

Letting A Simple Book Pre-Sell Your Prospects

Many professional recruiters are taking a low-key approach to network marketing recruiting by presenting it as a way to accumulate a retirement nest egg. The technique is motivating and simple.

First, you loan a copy of the book *How To Get Rich Without Winning The Lottery*. You can get a handful of these paperback books for less than $1.50 each, so stock up on plenty. The book explains how anyone can acquire wealth by using any of several methods suggested. Some of the methods suggested are:

1. Spending less than you earn and investing the difference.

2. Earning more through a part-time job and investing the difference.

3. Having a part-time business and investing the proceeds.

4. Collecting a network marketing check for what you are already doing, and then investing it.

Most readers immediately identify with one of the plans or examples and become very excited about the concept. They realize the more money they put aside, the faster they accumulate wealth and retirement. Allow your prospects about three days for reading the book before you return to pick it up.

When you pick up the book your prospect will probably be so impressed with its contents that he will want to keep it for his own personal library. At that time ask the question, "If there were a way to double or triple the amount you set aside, would you like to know about it?" The response is always, "You bet!" This is your lead into your network marketing Opportunity Presentation.

The selling point is that they can take the earnings from their network marketing business and add that to their early retirement fund. Now you'll see some real excitement in your prospects. This gives them a way to reach their financial wealth goals many times faster. For example, with only a couple hundred dollars extra part-time monthly income contributed to their retirement fund, your prospects could retire in 10-20 years.

This gives you long-term, secure distributors who are looking for a stable career with you.

This contrasts to the person who pushed to make his network marketing income equal his full-time job so he can quit working. When this person's earnings do not meet his expectations quick enough, he becomes discouraged and quits. This is not true of your distributors who are just looking for a steady income to invest on a permanent basis.

If you haven't read the book, don't prejudge this technique. This is one of the most powerful ways to build a solid group of doers.

Barter For Higher Personal Volumes

A network marketing vitamin distributor needed a shampoo and set at a local beauty salon. When her hair was finished and it was time to pay the $20, an idea popped into her mind. The beautician had mentioned that she got tired working on her feet all day, so the vitamin distributor offered to give her $20.00 worth of vitamins instead of cash.

Anxious to keep the distributor as a steady customer, the beautician agreed. The beautician normally could not afford a good vitamin program, but if the distributor would come regularly she could now accumulate all the vitamins she needed. Besides, why not earn vitamins instead of having an empty chair in front of her? The beautician's regular customers paid cash and covered her bills. An extra new customer for vitamins seemed like a good deal. All it cost was a little time, time that was presently empty.

The vitamin distributor returned home and did some calculations. The $20.00 of vitamins only cost her $15.00 wholesale. She also received a bonus of $5.00 (25%) because she was a supervisor and maintained a high volume. Her net cost was only $10.00, a savings of 50%!

If she could trade for many of her everyday needs she would receive the following benefits:

1. A savings of 50% on her purchases. It was like cutting her budget in half.

2. New customers who would not normally pay cash. Many people thought her vitamins were expensive and would not pay cash. However, they were willing to trade some goods, services, or free time for them. She could now attract customers with this marketing technique.

3. By trading for auto repair, bookkeeping, etc., she was increasing her volume of products ordered from the company. It was like earning a volume bonus on expenditures in her regular budget. It also helped her reach her monthly quotas.

4. By saving 50% on many budget items, she could now take that money and re-invest it in her business or put it into her savings account.

5. If her new customer experienced good results, many cash referrals could develop.

The approach she developed was simple.

(A) Try to find businesses that want more customers and are not too busy. If a business was operating at capacity with cash customers, they would not be enthusiastic about working overtime for vitamins. However, if an auto repair shop had to remain open eight hours a day and was only busy for six hours, they wouldn't mind filling those two non-productive hours with a trade customer.

(B) Don't interfere with their regular customers. Instead of saying, "I want it done now," say "Please fit this in when you are not busy."

(C) Remind the business that you can be a regular customer.

(D) Tell the business that you'll be a good advertiser for them. Promise to spread the word to help them get new customers.

Something For Nothing

What if one day we walked into our local bank and made the following proposition to the bank officer:

"I would like to deposit $100,000 into a Certificate of Deposit. I want to begin drawing interest on it immediately. However, I am not ready to make the deposit now, but you can start making the interest payments to me immediately."

The banker would probably say, "No way!" You must make the deposit before you can start earning the interest. As silly as this example sounds, we contact many prospects every month who wish for the same thing.

They want the rewards first before they deposit the effort.

Have you ever heard the following statements by distributors and distributor prospects?

- "I don't want to buy product this month. Let me wait until next month to see if I will have a big enough bonus check."

- "If I had a bigger bonus check, then I would get excited."

✍ "This sounds like a lot of hard work. It may take several months before I could reap the rewards."

✍ "Why should I pay for a meeting room for my group? Let them pay for it. They are the ones who are going to use it."

✍ "If you promise to build a big group for me, then I'll consider joining."

✍ "Let the company come out with a new advertising campaign that will get distributors flocking to my door. That is when I'll start working."

✍ "If my group was doing better, then I could afford to help them grow."

✍ "Why should I invest in products and sales aids? I haven't made any money yet."

The list can go on and on. People always seem to want something for nothing.

Wouldn't it be nice if companies paid us before we worked? Sure would. But let's be realistic. If we are going to make it as leaders, we must help our prospects and distributors understand that **reward follows effort.** There is no free lunch.

New Distributor Start-Up

It has been said, "If you don't know where you are going, any road will get you there." The problem with new distributors is they really don't know where they are going or how to get there. The bigger problem is when their sponsor doesn't know how to get them there.

Let's begin in the start-up when the sponsor sells them a new distributor kit and no product. We all know you can't sell from an empty wagon so why do we wish to handicap our new recruit? He will need product immediately for four different areas of his business.

1. **Personal Use.** The surest way to learn and be sold upon the product. If our recruit does not believe in the product strongly enough to use it, why did we even sponsor him in the first place? He should be his own best customer.

2. **Retail sales.** He should have enough product on hand to make a few retail sales. How does it look to a potential customer when your new recruit approaches him to buy, but doesn't even

have enough confidence in his product to bring some for instant delivery? It's as though he expects his customer not to buy. But even if he does make a sale, all his profit is burned up in gas traveling back and forth to his house, his sponsor's house to get the product, and again back to the retail customer. The purpose of the business is to make a profit, not to support Texaco or Shell. Besides, would you continue to shop at a grocery store if they told you that you could get your products in a week or so?

3. **Samples**. If your product lends itself to samples, you must have some on hand to set a good personal example, i.e., leadership. If you happen to be in a food program, give away or sell prospects a small two or three dollar unit of food for them to try and report on. If you're in a cleaner company . . . use a small size of a popular cleaner, etc.

4. **New Distributor Start-Up.** When you start a new distributor, he needs some immediate product that night. If you plan to start several new distributors, you need to have plenty of extra products on hand. These products are to jump-start your new distributor until he receives his personal order from the company. If your new recruit plans to sponsor several people right away, he needs a good-sized inventory to get him off to a good start.

A big motivating factor for initial inventory for new recruits is that they will keep the business on their mind if they have just spent $200 or $300 for product. Of course you give them a money-back guarantee, as your purpose is to help them get started fast, not make money off an incompetent slow-starter. We just want everyone to have the best start possible.

If their funds are short, offer to take a postdated check. Getting product into their hands is crucial to their success. After all, it is hardly worth sponsoring someone who does not have or is not willing to open a checking account. So offer to take a postdated check if they cannot afford a good start-up order.

To sum it up, our new distributors will only earn money on moving products. Let's give our new distributors the best chance possible to become successful.

Benefits

Some innovative advertising for new recruits has been surfacing recently. Rather than concentrate on the main theme or benefit of their business opportunity, sales leaders are pinpointing specific benefits and highlighting them to attract new recruits. The hope is to locate a person with a specific need for this benefit and then converting him to the business opportunity. For example, one ad reads: Need a new car? Don't pay thousands for a down payment. Don't pay high monthly lease payments. Receive a new car from us every two years and earn $1,000 to $1,500 monthly part-time. Call (xxx) xxx-xxxx.

This network marketing company offers a car on lease to its sales leaders who achieve a group sales volume of $5,000 for five consecutive months. The prospect answers the ad, believing he may get a company car and might be working as a car lease agent.

Reality is that the prospect will have to build a network marketing group to $5,000 monthly and at that time will receive his automobile. The approach works well with people who have a fear of network marketing and are highly motivated to get a car.

The success, of course, is entirely up to the sponsor in convincing him that network marketing is a viable business opportunity and a great way to earn his car. A good approach to the prospect is to have a pre-set plan that is easily understood and appears easy enough to be motivating.

One plan presented to a new prospect was the following:

We carry a fine line of various products that you normally buy at your local store. By changing your purchasing habits and those of a few of your friends, let me show you how you will earn $700.00 a month and a "no cost" lease car.

Every month you will purchase $100.00 of product from us. This amount will be conveniently deducted from your checking account. (Automatic deductions from checking accounts make the purchase or quota painless and easy.) You may pick up the products you need at any time during the month at your convenience. I will then help you sign up two of your friends to do the same. We then will help each of them to sign up two of their friends, etc. No one person will have to sign up more than two friends. After all, everyone knows at least two people.

Your group will then look like this: 2 first level, 4 second level, 6 third level, 16 fourth level and 32 fifth level distributors for a grand total of 63 distributors. At $100.00 volume each, that is $6,300.00 total volume; more than plenty to qualify for your car. And all you have to do is sponsor two people and change their purchasing habits. Your part-time income would be in excess of $700.00 and you would have a "no cost" lease car for two years. And by the way, your distributors can qualify for the same car and part-time income that you do.

The interesting part of the above presentation is that the philosophy of network marketing, the company background, product line and benefits, and even the marketing plan were barely covered. Only the prospect's car and how to get it was presented. All the rest of our normal presentation was discarded.

Another widely advertised benefit is health insurance. The ad headline reads, "Is your health insurance too expensive?" or "Group health insurance rates for individuals."

Some network marketing companies offer reduced rate or free health insurance for their top sales leaders. The prospect may be pleasantly surprised that he can get cheaper health insurance and earn extra money at the same time. It's making the health insurance free plus a profit.

How about trips? Does your company offer travel incentives? How many people do you know who could never afford a first class vacation or who felt there are better places for their money? A truly first class vacation paid for by your network marketing company could be the very motivating reason that they join.

How hard is it to get someone excited about a free all-expense paid trip to Acapulco, Hawaii, Europe, etc.? What if you had a plan laid out where all they had to do was use and sell a certain amount of product and sponsor just a few people to do the same? You'd be surprised what someone would do for a one week first class vacation.

As network marketing becomes more popular every year, new approaches must be used to reach those people who have only a bit of knowledge and have made a negative evaluation based on too little information. This is a sizable market of untapped potential that could be yours for the asking. What benefits does your company offer? Tax benefits, car, trips, insurance, recognition, jewelry, or ?????

How To Work In Circles

Did you ever notice how some network marketers seem to work extremely hard and get absolutely nowhere? It almost makes you cry to see such effort go unrewarded. Many times these unfortunate souls are in our downline and look to us to solve their dilemma. Let's take a case.

Marvin Mover is the epitome of a salesman. As a matter of fact, he looks like your next superstar. Marvin has great work habits and consistency. Every day he sets three recruiting appointments and sponsors at least one new person. It doesn't take long to see that in 30 days Marvin will have at least 30 distributors in his group.

The problem is that his group is producing no volume. Most of his new recruits don't even place an initial order, and those who do, won't re-order. Marvin is working hard, but going in circles and getting nowhere. And the worst part is that this whole situation is frustrating for you. You see your potential superstar getting discouraged by the lack of tangible results — no volume.

Let's define the problem.

Marvin Mover is a salesman. Marvin is busy **convincing** every prospect with his highly refined sales skills. He is most anxious to "make the sale" and is happy to get his prospect's name on the dotted line on the distributor agreement. Unfortunately, Marvin stops selling his prospect right there. He is failing to get a **commitment** from his prospect to work the business. He leaves the prospect alone to make his own decision on his personal goals, his plan of activity, and his commitment of effort to make the business work for him. What could possibly be worse?

The new recruit has no experience on which to base his decisions and will probably act like 95% of the general populace; he will fail to make a decision or commitment on his own unless someone who is a leader holds his hand and helps him.

Marvin Mover has avoided the most important part of the sale, getting the COMMITMENT. An example of Marvin's closing remarks on his recruiting presentation might go like this: "Mr. New Recruit, I am sure glad you have decided to join our wonderful organization. You should make an order of some products to get started this month, so I am leaving you a price list and catalog to look over. Please think of some people that you can recruit so you can have some distributors in your group. Just call me if you have any problems. By the way, there is a big meeting planned for the last Saturday of this month. I plan to be there. See if you can make it."

Marvin has just left the entire commitment process up to Mr. New Recruit. What a mistake! Many times we do the same as Marvin for several reasons.

1. We are so excited about the successful recruiting presentation that we pack our bags and go home to rejoice.

2. We are afraid that if we ask for a commitment at this time, Mr. New Recruit might rethink his decision and quit.

3. We suffer from masochistic, suicidal, and failure complexes and decided that failing to get commitments is the easiest way to achieve our goals.

Of the three reasons, number two is most often the cause of failing to get a commitment.

Logically, when is the best time to get a commitment? At the initial presentation when the prospect's enthusiasm for the business is at its highest peak? Or several days later after he has cooled down about the opportunity? Certainly it would seem getting the commitment at the initial presentation would be best. Waiting until later forces you to rekindle his enthusiasm before you can begin to get a commitment.

The reason most network marketers wait until a second meeting to get the commitment is that they do not want to jeopardize the initial sale, getting the prospect into the business. This "bird in the hand" theory is to make sure he is in the business solidly before you begin to push him into a commitment. Unfortunately this strategy backfires.

Let's say that during the initial presentation you ask Mr. New Recruit for a commitment to purchase product, set a couple of recruiting appointments, and to attend that next big rally.

Mr. New Recruit replies, "No way, if I have to do all that, I don't want to be involved. You might as well just rip up my application and throw it away."

If this was his reply at the initial presentation when his enthusiasm was at his highest, just think of how negative his reply would have been a few days later when his feeling for the business were much less positive. Isn't it to our advantage to find out now if we have a good new recruit before we spend a lot of time and effort on a useless, non-producing recruit?

It appears that we have EVERYTHING TO GAIN and NOTHING TO LOSE by getting the commitment right away at the initial presentation. Why wait until later when we will only be wasting his time and ours? Let's get the commitment now.

Catching The Big Fish

Raymond and June Trout were hard-working, moderately successful network marketers. Over the years their consistent effort had won them the loyalty of several good downline distributors. Raymond and June were also well-liked in their community.

Unfortunately, network marketing had not been profitable for the Trouts in recent years. Their last network marketing company had gone out of business and the previous company had good products, but the Trouts had some conflict with their upline sponsors. So the Trouts had given up on network marketing about a year ago and joined the ranks of network marketing burnouts. Raymond continued working his regular job and June stayed home with the children.

Across town lived Big Al. Big Al had just finished training a new distributor and was looking for a new potential recruit.

The Trouts certainly would be good candidates because they previously showed their desire to become successful by their hard work with their previous distributors. Big Al felt their training in network marketing was deficient and that was the one missing link to their success. Big Al knew his on-the-job training would make the

Trouts a big fish in network marketing. They had the contacts; Big Al had the skill.

Only one problem remained. The Trouts never wanted to be associated with a network marketing company again. Their last experiences were not profitable and they just didn't want to spin their wheels again.

But the Trouts would be a big catch, so Big Al began to look for a motivating reason for them to again get involved with network marketing.

Being a one-car family meant June Trout had to wait for Raymond to return home to use the car. This could be motivating, but most network marketing programs require several months of qualification and some pretty high volumes to get a company car. It would be hard to convince the Trouts to work hard for several months for only a chance of getting an extra car.

On Monday morning, Big Al went to the local car dealership and rented a nice little sports car. Big Al drove the car over to June Trout's home and stopped in to visit. He explained to June his network marketing program and how he would personally mentor them to success. Big Al assured June that she and Raymond would probably not be interested in the opportunity even though they would earn $200 to $300 extra monthly with his help. Big Al just wanted to leave the information so June could talk it over with her husband.

When Big Al was ready to leave, he asked June to give him a ride home in the sports car. Big Al explained that if they became involved with his program, the extra income would easily make the payments on the rented car he drove over.

Just so June could see the benefits of joining, Big Al told her that the car was hers to use for the next two days. If she wanted to keep the car, all she had to do was to convince Raymond to join her in the program. When June dropped Big Al off at his house she was already sold on the idea of having her own car for shopping and school errands. Big Al thanked her for the ride and said he would stop by in two days.

Big Al knew that once June was exposed to the convenience and flexibility of her own car, there would be no stopping June in her efforts in network marketing.

By the time Raymond arrived home from work, June had already made the prospect list for Raymond and Big Al to visit.

Life's Law

"Fear Of Loss Is Greater Than The Desire For Gain."
—*Big Al*

We would all like to change people.

However, we can get better results by working with people and accepting them just the way they are. If people could really be changed it would probably be a miracle. Want proof?

There are almost 100 million marriages in this country. In every marriage one spouse or both is trying to change the other. The husband was a slob before they got married, so the wife felt that once they were married she could change him, etc. In the almost 100 million marriages, there has been no evidence of any spouse changing the other. People just don't want to be changed.

Well, if people don't want to be changed, don't you think that we could get better results by working with them just the way they are?

So how are we going to **motivate** people? Are we going to use all those neat ways we read about in all the motivation books? Most of those ways change their attitude. We should change their priorities. We should get them to see the bigger picture when they want only to see the little picture. We should try to get them to change their habits, etc.

We all know that these techniques have very limited success because **PEOPLE DO NOT WANT TO CHANGE.**

What can we do to motivate people? Just remember that people naturally put forth great effort to prevent losses in their lives.

For example, John Average gets a parking ticket. Rather than LOSE the $17 to pay the fine, John takes the morning off to go to court to get the ticket dismissed. No way is John going to lose $17.

How much did John save? In reality, he really lost. Let's take a tally:

$45	Lost pay by missing work that morning.
$ 5	Spent on gas driving to and from court.
<u>$ 5</u>	Parking fees to park car while in court (John was not going to get another ticket.)
$55	Total spent to avoid losing $17!

John was motivated to make a tremendous effort to avoid loss, a perfect example of FEAR OF LOSS.

Another example: Sally had just checked out of the motel an hour earlier and was about 50 miles down the road. Suddenly she remembered that she had left her $20 watch on the dresser of her motel room. Rather than continue on her trip, guess what Sally does. Of course, she wastes two hours returning to the motel plus spending the gas for the round trip, definite FEAR OF LOSS.

On the other side of the coin, Sally could have continued on her trip, made a sale or two during the same two hours lost, and made twice as much money. Was her DESIRE FOR GAIN greater than her FEAR OF LOSS?

No, Sally was **motivated** to avoid loss.

Sam uses all his weekends to mow the grass and paint his house. He could hire a local high school boy to do the same work for only a few dollars. Here's another example of FEAR OF LOSS. Sam just doesn't want to part with

the money. Sam could take a part-time job at the local drugstore during the weekend and earn three times the money he would pay the local boy for yard work and painting.

That's a perfect example of this law. Sam won't make the effort to gain but will work hard personally all weekend to avoid loss.

Larry has just lost his girlfriend. To win her back, Larry sends flowers, candy, presents, calls regularly, etc.

A tremendous effort that was totally absent until his girlfriend left. Larry did not like the loss and was motivated to extraordinary effort to prevent the loss. His FEAR OF LOSS was greater than his DESIRE FOR GAIN since he never expended this effort to improve their relationship when things were going well.

So how do we apply this powerful observation of how people are motivated? Let's accept the way people are and motivate them through the principle:

"FEAR OF LOSS IS GREATER THAN THE DESIRE FOR GAIN."

Instead of pleading, cajoling, bribing and attempting to get our lazy first level distributor to work and order product, let's take a different tactic, FEAR OF LOSS.

We are going to personally sponsor a couple of distributors and place them under our lazy first level distributor. In order for our lazy first level distributor to collect his override bonuses, he must order product. If he doesn't order product, he will lose the bonus he would have earned on these distributors.

Now just what do you think your lazy first level distributor will do?

He will make the effort to order product to prevent the loss of bonus due him. Have we motivated him? Yes.

Is his FEAR OF LOSS GREATER THAN HIS DESIRE FOR GAIN? Yes. We have previously been unsuccessful in motivating him with promises of riches, etc., if he would only order product and get started in the business.

Can we apply this principle elsewhere in our business? Yes. We are only limited by our imagination.

The Dairy Farm
Syndrome

Every network marketing distributor has posed these questions sometime in his network marketing career: "How do I get more volume in my group?" or "How can I increase those monthly bonus checks?"

By examining the options available, only two courses of action seem possible for achieving the desired results. Let us take a look at course of action Number One.

1. Train the present distributor force to increase volume.

This option is taken by almost every network marketing distributor for several reasons. Logic dictates that through proper training we can upgrade each of our present active distributors to personal higher volume standards.

If each active distributor did as much personal volume as we did because of better product knowledge, if each active distributor understood and loved the products as we do, if each active distributor would use and sell more, and if each active distributor could learn the sales and prospecting skills we have acquired over our careers, our volume could double or even triple overnight.

In addition, if our training could motivate all those non-motivated distributors that we have accumulated over our career, just think of the tremendous potential increase in our group's volume. The only thing holding us back could be the training of our distributors.

So we decide to institute a product training program for three Thursday nights in a row. At least that much time is needed to learn the ingredients, test reports, testimonials, and company literature. We have homework, weekly tests, and demonstrations. Those attending are our core group of distributors who always show up every meeting, most times without a new guest or recruit, but they appreciate the new insight into the product line. As a matter of fact they are so impressed with our training that they insist we immediately move on to the retail sales training we promised.

Our retail training is scheduled for Saturdays from 9 a.m. to 2 p.m. for four Saturdays in a row. We want to build solid closing skills, learn to handle objections, AIDA formulas, facts, features, benefits, etc. We incorporate role playing, sales contests, memorize product line presentations, etc. Our newly trained group is so good that you can't say "Hello" without them putting a trial close on you.

Now our group is ready for a full-fledged recruiting workshop. Wouldn't it be nice to use all these new sales skills on some potential new distributor prospects? On Monday nights we schedule a 7 p.m. to 10 p.m. recruiting class for the next five weeks. We will cover prospecting, closing, openers, interest steps, advertising, direct mail, closing and starting our new distributors. After all, what better sponsor could a new distributor have than a well-trained, mature pro in our business!

After our recruiting training, we notice our graduates are not producing new distributors on a regular basis, if at all. It appears that they are setting a poor personal example and could use some leadership training. We employ a consultant who charges our distributors $375 per person to put them through an intensified, two-weekend seminar to teach them the principles that make great leaders. After all, how can they build a large organization if they are unable to lead?

Then it finally hits us.

We have developed a mature force of old-time distributors, who know everything about the product, can give credible presentations to a new recruit, have excellent sales skills, and know how to be a good leader, but are not motivated to do a thing.

With this fact staring us in the face, we truly see that all of our previous training has been for naught, wasted totally. All the skills in the world mean nothing if our distributors are not motivated to go out, overcome their fears, and do something. What we have is a group of professional students, always going to classes and training so they won't have to go out in the real world to do the work.

And why should they? In all the training classes they never get rejection and are surrounded by positive people. It's much more fun.

Finally we have identified our problem. We have a tired old mature distributor force of professional meeting-goers who enjoy the fellowship and social life our business offers. They are so afraid of success that they are constantly going to seminars, workshops, classes, etc., to keep themselves busy so they will not have to face the real world with its objections and rejections.

Solution . . . forget and throw away all our training and instead have one really good training on motivation.

If we can get our people motivated, results would follow. After all, we have seen many new distributors with no sales, recruiting, or product skills go out and build large businesses because they were motivated to do it. Our group of loyal groupies lacks the motivation to overcome their fears. Therefore they do nothing. They enjoy going to so many meetings there is no time left to go out and use the information and skills learned. We are basically training them to death.

If motivation is our solution, we will go out and get the best motivational speaker we can find and book him or her into an all-day Saturday affair to really psyche our troops up, to get them to realize their potential, to believe in themselves, to go out and do it!

The big day arrives and the only people there are our core group of over-trained groupies. However, this time things are different. Our group is standing on chairs, screaming success slogans, making new commitments, setting goals, getting the spirit and really getting motivated. They are slapping each other on the back saying how great they feel, how great everyone there is, and believing with conviction they now are truly going to the top. Our formerly tired, mature groupies are now goal-oriented, motivated doers, and just can't wait to leave and go out and do it.

Saturday evening they go home and re-define their goals. They spread the word with their family that finally they can expect big things from the business.

Sunday being a day of rest, our newly motivated distributors make good use of the time mapping their plan of action and re-listening to a good motivational tape.

Monday is a workday, but they get home and the first challenge is who to approach first. After reviewing their prospect list, they determine Fred and Joe would be good first targets. Fred reminds him that he has been invited at least 15 times to an opportunity meeting and is serious about his non-interest.

Undaunted, our distributor jumps up and down and yells, "I feel great!" and for good measure jumps off a chair or two. We certainly are not going to let Fred ruin our motivation.

The next phone calls goes to Joe who says he can't meet with us tonight because the big Monday Night Football game is coming on in 30 minutes. Our motivated distributor takes the hint, and decides to watch the game also, since he had completely forgotten about this important game in his goal-setting excitement.

Tuesday night brings the same results. One or two phone calls to some old prospects confirms his suspicions that no one is really interested in the business.

Wednesday is church night and on Thursday, everyone is planning for the weekend.

Weekends are definitely not the time to recruit as people are spending time with their families and enjoying the two days off their jobs.

Course of action Number One does not produce the desired results after careful examination of the facts. What is the real solution to the problem of "How to get more volume?" Next chapter, we'll look at a successful solution to the Dairy Farm Syndrome.

The Dairy Farm Syndrome (Part II)

The major problem of network marketing leaders is that they believe that by squeezing harder, you can get more milk. **The real solution to get more milk is to get more cows.** Statistics over the last 30 years prove that the only way to increase group volume is to get a larger group. Squeezing a few extra dollars from your present distributors will never get an appreciable increase in group volume.

Ten times the results can be accomplished by using your effort to locate new distributors rather than squeezing a few drops more out of your present people.

Why don't leaders spend this valuable time looking for distributors?

Fear of rejection.

It is easy to spend time teaching your present group and getting compliments that you are so smart and wonderful. Unfortunately, this doesn't improve your business. It only gives you a good warm feeling. If you are in business for a good warm feeling, this would be nice; but if you are looking for a business profit and to increase volume, this continuous training is a cruel joke on both you and your distributors.

Sponsoring new recruits is not as pleasant. You suffer rejection when they say "No." Many times you feel that if you just could go back to the sheltered environment of your present, pre-sold group, you would feel happier. It is not so easy to go out and look for strangers, convince them to set an appointment, and then to sell them on the wonderful opportunity and your personal leadership.

Logic is easy to state, but hard to implement. Of course, we should all stop visiting and socializing with our present group of distributors. Sure, we should go out on the street and get new distributors. More cows mean more milk.

However, we have several factors going against us. No leads, fears, no credibility with strangers, little sales experience, and no plan for success.

The solution is the "Two-on-One" sales presentation where our distributor makes the appointment and we make the presentation. The distributor contacts a friend or acquaintance and we make the presentation. We do not suffer the loss of confidence by receiving constant rejection, so we are in a good state of mind to make the presentation. All our distributor has to do is make the appointment and sit back and watch. This is the power of the system as it overcomes the fears and problems of cold recruiting, ("One on One.")

Another important factor in getting new recruits is that new recruits have enthusiasm. It is impossible to get old pros excited and enthusiastic. They have been around and have seen it all. They have already approached all their friends with their initial excitement and will normally just sit in a holding pattern of mediocrity.

How many times have we seen an unskilled, brand new distributor outperform the old pro just on his enthusiasm and excitement? Want to put new life into your group? Get new distributors. They will increase the entire group's activity and excitement.

Groups grow by spurts or by campaigns. You have to get the momentum going, but once started, the group will grow geometrically. We have all seen a group explode in size when everyone is excited and confident. And the confidence keeps growing as people bring in more and more people fueling the fire of the group.

The secret is how to start this fire or sponsoring campaign, instead of plodding along just getting one or two new distributors a week. Our goal is to set off a recruiting explosion or a movement to cause a mass sponsoring to occur.

To summarize, don't waste your time overtraining and socializing with your distributors. The only true route to building bigger volume is to get more distributors, not by squeezing your present distributors harder.

To get more milk, get more cows!

The Case Of The Missing Retirement

Joe Office Worker was 58 years old and only now began to seriously think about retirement. Throughout his working career he never saved or planned for his upcoming retirement and now was suddenly struck with the problem of very little time — and a lot to accomplish. Joe had to produce a retirement income in just seven years.

Fortunately Joe had something to start with. His company pension plan offered $550 a month. While this was just a pittance, it was better than nothing.

Joe wondered about all those years he believed that the company would take care of him in his retirement. What a joke! Seven years from now when he is ready to retire, $550 probably won't even pay the utility bills and real estate taxes.

Joe would also be eligible for Social Security benefits when he retired. His benefits were calculated to be $750 per month. "At least I'll be getting something back for all those years I paid in," Joe thought to himself.

Now a $1,300 a month retirement is not a lot of money, but it is more than many people have when they retire. Joe decided that after food, auto expenses, rent or

mortgage payments, etc., $1,300 would barely provide minimum needs. "How can I save and make up for lost time?" Joe thought.

Joe decided to go into a part-time business of his own. He became a distributor for a network marketing company and, while not very successful, he did manage to net about $800 every month.

Joe systematically saved this for one year and used his $9,600 savings as a 10% down payment on a $96,000 house next door. The house was rented for $1,200 a month and after taxes, insurance, and minor expenses, there was $1,000 left to service the $86,000 mortgage.

Joe had obtained the mortgage at 7% interest and decided to pay if off in **six years** so that the house would be free and clear of all debt when he reached 65 years of age.

To do this it would require a monthly payment of $1,500. Joe took the $1,000 net from the rent and added $500 from his network marketing monthly check for a total of $1,500 a month payment.

At the end of six years the house was fully paid for. Since real estate in Joe's neighborhood appreciated at about 9% a year, the house was now worth $130,000. Joe now sold the house to a friend for no money down, and gave his friend a 20-year, 8% mortgage with payments of $1,100 monthly for principal and interest. Now Joe's financial retirement picture looked a whole lot brighter.

Company Pension Plan	$ 550
Social Security	750
Mortgage from House	1,100
Network marketing Income	800
TOTAL INCOME	**$3,200**

Joe decided to continue his part-time business after he retired. He enjoyed the activity and could always find a way to spend the money. At a retirement income of $3,280 a month Joe lived comfortably ever after.

Network Marketing Leader's Note: Just think of the retirement income Joe could have accumulated if he had started just 8 or 10 years earlier. By reinvesting the income of each house purchased, Joe could easily have retired on $50,000 per year or more.

Remember: Many new distributors never realize that only a small success of $800 monthly income, if invested wisely, can mean financial independence in just a few years. You don't have to be a superstar in network marketing to reach financial security.

Strawberry Fields Forever

The real secret in selling is relating in terms that your prospect will understand. How many times have you seen intelligent salesmen use high-tech terminology that sounds impressive to the prospect? While this sounds impressive, most times the prospect fails to buy because he does not understand the entire presentation.

We must remember that if any part of our presentation fails to be clear, the natural tendency of the prospect is to delay a decision because of "fear of the unknown."

Examples of this in network marketing to new prospects could be the following terms (the prospect's interpretations in parenthesis):

➤ Downline *(an event to happen later on)*

➤ PV *(a rare disease as in, "Be careful not to catch a lot of PV's")*

➤ BV *(a more powerful strain of the disease)*

➤ Breakaway *(leaving the network marketing business to do something else)*

➤ Sponsor *(free will donations to starving children overseas)*

➤ Bonuses *(the turkey given to company employees at Christmas)*

➤ Distributor *(the part that breaks and your car won't start)*

➤ Wholesaler *(the meat packing plant on the other end of town)*

➤ Overrides *(4th gear on an automatic transmission).*

Any of the above words can be used in presentations. However, we must give proper explanations and be aware of our prospect's difficulty in translating our true meaning. If you want to have a little fun, attend a group opportunity meeting and listen to the jargon used by the speaker. Notice the blank stare of the new prospects in the room. You'll probably be the only one laughing in the room, but at least you'll see a dramatic demonstration of bad communication.

All this, of course, brings us to **strawberries.**

The strawberry story is an excellent way to relate how network marketing works to a beginner. Many times a beginner is reluctant to join because he questions the legitimacy or the legality of network marketing distribution. The strawberry story puts him at ease because it shows network marketing as an alternative way of distributing products to the familiar retail distribution system.

The story:

Let's say we want to buy strawberries from our local store. How did they get there?

First, the strawberries were picked at a small farm in California and sold to the local co-op. Next, the co-op sold them to a large national distributor. The national distributor sells the strawberries to regional brokers who, in turn, resell them at a profit to local jobbers. The local jobbers sell the strawberries to large warehouses for the local grocery chains who then distribute them to the local grocery stores who mark up the price another 30-40% for overhead such as employee salaries, rent, advertising, insurance, utilities, inventory shrinkage, etc.

Each person along the way covers his overhead and adds on a profit. So while the strawberries may have cost only 25 cents in the field, the final price at the store is $1.00. This is known as the retail distribution method of marketing.

An alternative way of distribution is direct marketing or network marketing. Here the farmers (or manufacturers) sell the strawberries directly to the network marketing company. The network marketing company sells the strawberries directly to their distributors at wholesale. The distributors benefit by being able to purchase strawberries for their personal use at wholesale and can also make extra money by selling them to retail customers at retail. This is a more direct way of marketing products, and by cutting out all the middle man profits, the network marketing company is able to pass these savings on to their distributors for additional profits called bonuses.

Bonuses work like this. If you bought strawberries at your local grocery store and liked them so much that you told your neighbor, your local store would receive additional sales because of your word-of-mouth advertising.

The store, in its appreciation of your work, would then send you in the mail the next day a word-of-mouth advertising bonus check. Not very likely. The store has already spent its advertising budget in the local newspaper so there is nothing left for you.

But in network marketing it is all different!

If you liked the strawberries you purchased at wholesale from your network marketing company, then told your neighbor about them, and your neighbor became a distributor and purchased strawberries at wholesale from your network marketing company, you get a bonus! The network marketing company will give you a bonus for your effort that resulted in their increased sales.

That is why so many people are excited about network marketing. For doing what comes naturally (sharing a good deal) we get paid bonuses. Retail stores just can't compete when people find out about the tremendous advantages of network marketing. After all, if you liked the strawberries and told your neighbor, which would you choose:

Getting paid for it by a network marketing company or not getting paid by your local store?

The choice is clear: *Network marketing or direct marketing is a better deal for us.*

How To Make Successful Recruiting Presentations

"It's not enough to just memorize a successful recruiting presentation," said Big Al, "You must understand the principles and the psychology behind great presentations.

"In order to do that, let's look at a presentation given by someone else. Obviously, we can't all sit in on a two-on-one presentation, so let's attend a business opportunity meeting given by a leader with another company. We want to watch someone who is confident, can speak in front of a group, has attained some degree of success, and would generally be considered in the top 5%."

That Monday night Big Al and Distributor Joe attended an opportunity meeting for "Wonderful Products." They both sat in the back row so they could take careful notes of both the speaker and the crowd reaction.

They chose this meeting because it had a reputation of being exciting and the very best in town. With notepads in hand, they patiently awaited as the meeting started 35 minutes late to allow for latecomers. Big Al mentioned that starting late is really punishing the distributors who come on time while rewarding those who are tardy. Finally, the meeting started.

The opening speaker introduced himself and immediately began to tell the audience how great he was. He mentioned that he was in the top 5% of all people because he thought like a winner. Obviously, the people in the audience were losers because they were not presently distributors for this wonderful company and they needed to have their thinking changed . . .

After 20 minutes of explaining why the listeners were only sheep being led to a financial slaughter, the speaker finally got around to naming the company and began telling about its wonderful founders.

One founder grew up in a log cabin and suffered defeat after defeat. Only through superhuman effort was he able to overcome these hardships and develop his own philosophy on life. This philosophy was to become the backbone of the company and the only reason for the company was to share this wonderful knowledge with others. The company was not in business to make a profit, but to change the minds of America.

The other founder's ancestry was revealed in explicit detail for 10 minutes, and then his long list of academic achievements was read. His long journeys to ancient tombs and cultures, his knowledge of ancient manuscripts, and his elaborate test techniques were cited. One lady in the crowd stood up and cheered with tears in her eyes, explaining how the products had changed her life. At least this woke up the audience.

After another 15 minutes of homage to the founders, the speaker invited present distributors to come to the front of the room to explain the products and share their experiences.

The first distributor said he really hadn't been a distributor long enough to try the products, but knew of someone who had taken them and recovered from cancer, senility and hardening of the arteries within one week by swallowing 42 tablets a day.

The next distributor told how you could make millions in just a few short weeks in this wonderful pyramid concept. In fact, you didn't even have to use or like the products, all you had to do is to get others to invest in a kit and everyone would get rich. A few members of the audience clapped loudly and yelled, "Go for it!"

The next distributor said he didn't like the taste of the product but felt it helped enough people so it wouldn't be a problem for anyone in the business. About that time a few guests in the audience looked at their watches, and quietly crept out the back door.

The next distributor told of his personal experience. He had been blind, deaf, crippled and next to death until he drank Wonderful's Super Juice. In two weeks' time he was completely healed and had qualified for the Olympic marathon. Two "business types" in the audience rolled

their eyes and looked at their potential sponsor thinking, "What is this?" The distributor then proceeded to ask the audience to sing the "Wonderful Products" healing song.

Finally, the next speaker arose and announced that he was going to talk about the marketing plan. After 90 minutes of questionable information, the audience was relieved to see the meeting finally get to the point. However, several people did leave because of other commitments or baby-sitting problems. The marketing plan of Wonderful Products was revealed to the remaining group.

First, a person becomes qualified advisor counselor at captain level. After accumulating "wonderful points" the person could receive 4% of the 6% training bonus on unqualified private non-advisor distributors on every non-calendar month.

When a person reached a total BV of 60% of his personal group's PV, not counting bonus product points, he then could move to a 70% level of net profit on single case sales. The "blue moon" convention points were completely different, though. In that case a person would come into the program as a non-qualified distributor and qualify through a unique "general direct supervisory plan." Finally, this decision should be made immediately as the charter month was about to end tomorrow.

After 30 minutes of detailed explanation of the finer points of Wonderful Products marketing plan, the speaker invited another person to the front of the room to tell his personal story.

Ten minutes later this speaker was completely confused where he was, so he called the meeting to an end and thanked the few remaining hard core distributors for coming. They all smiled and said what a great meeting it was and retired to the local bar to discuss strategy for their next great meeting.

1. INDUSTRY
2. COMPANY
3. PRODUCTS
4. **TRAINING**
5. MARKETING PLAN

The Answer
To Inefficient
Recruiting Presentations

Big Al and Distributor Joe went to a local coffee shop to discuss the two-hour opportunity meeting they had just attended. "Absolutely amazing!" commented Distributor Joe. "I have never seen a more disorganized and unprofessional excuse for a business presentation. I didn't know whether to be sick or to laugh. The most intelligent people at the meeting were the guests. At least they had the common sense to leave halfway through the presentation. I can see why there is really no competition in network marketing. Anyone who takes just a little time to learn the basics can leave the majority miles behind."

Big Al nodded in agreement and said, "Joe, you have watched me give many a presentation and have given plenty on your own with your own group. You have been copying my basic presentation, but now is a good time to learn why we have structured our presentation the way we have.

"As you know, our presentation takes only 25-30 minutes and goes right to the core of the information the new prospect needs to make an intelligent decision whether to join or not. You may have noticed that our presentations have five key sections. Each key section is designed to answer one of the five key questions that every prospect has in order to make the decision to join. Let's review them so that you may better understand the science of professional network marketing business presentations."

SECTION 1: THE INDUSTRY

Our prospects will want to know what kind of industry we are in. They may have a particular aversion to certain industries such as insurance or real estate. We can answer this first question in their mind very easily. We simply tell them we are in the multi-level marketing or network marketing industry. There are two types of prospects, those who understand what network marketing is and those who don't.

For those familiar with network marketing, we have just answered their question and we can go quickly on to Section Two. For those who don't understand what network marketing is, we simply tell them the strawberry story. This story legitimizes the direct marketing concept and makes them feel comfortable with this alternative way of getting products and services to the public. We certainly want our prospects to be relaxed, don't we?

Section 1 of our presentation should only take three or four minutes at the most.

SECTION 2: THE COMPANY

Our prospect is not interested in a complete financial audit, the number of square feet in the executive washroom, the founder's mother's ancestry, the type of credentials of the quality control foreman, or the quality of paper used in the shipping and receiving room. His real desire is to know just the name of the company, if its management has some experience, and if the company is growing and has good plans for the future. In other words, if they are the good guys or the bad guys.

Too many presentations get carried away with a lot of credibility statistics that should be saved later for training. At this point of our new prospect's career, he just wants to know a few facts, not the company's entire history. His questions about the company can usually be answered in about one minute.

SECTION 3: THE PRODUCTS

Too many times the excited new distributor tells the new prospect what excites the new distributor, not what the prospect wants and needs to hear. When a new distributor gets started he is usually totally sold on his products. In his excitement he feels that the new prospect must listen to every testimonial, every test data report, and every feature of every individual product his company carries. This process can take many hours and usually puts the prospect to sleep if he can't find the energy to get away.

What the prospect really wants to know is, "Is there a market for the products? Will they sell?" Our entire product presentation should center not on the price, quality and test reports of the product, but on how people are using them and enjoying them now! We must answer the prospect's question. Sure, the other factors are important, but let's be professional and answer the question that will help the prospect decide if this business opportunity is for him.

Our product presentation should take about five to eight minutes. We are just giving an overview of individual products or product lines, not a complete product training workshop.

SECTION 4: TRAINING

This is the difference between professional recruiting presentations and those pathetic amateur attempts to present the business opportunity. Have you ever wondered why the following scenario happens?

A new distributor prospect sits through an entire meeting for an hour. At the end of the meeting he turns to his prospective sponsor and says, "Boy, those products are really great, and that marketing plan sure looks like the way to financial security. The amount of money to be made in this business is phenomenal! By the way, I am not going to join."

Why does this happen? Simple.

The person giving the presentation forgot to answer the most important question of the entire meeting: CAN I DO IT?

Our new prospect would certainly want all the benefits offered by our program, but he has never been in network marketing before, or has been previously unsuccessful at it. Therefore, we must answer his question, "Can I do it?" if we are to sponsor him into our program. We do this by explaining our training program.

Our training program consists of the literature, books, tapes, etc. available from the company. Also available are the many local training meetings in his area. We strongly encourage him to attend to BEGIN his learning process but this is only the first part of our training.

PART TWO is the "On-The-Job" training. We ask him to only set a few appointments and watch or observe while we sponsor new distributors into his organization. We are building his group while he is watching! What could be easier for him? Our new prospect will now feel more at ease knowing that he can attend training and observe his sponsor building his organization. Our new prospect will now realize that this is a business that he can do. With this assurance our prospect is ready to go with our program even before he hears about the money.

More distributors are recruited during these vital five minutes of training explanation than all other parts of the presentation combined.

SECTION 5: MARKETING PLAN

The last five or ten minutes of our presentation should be dedicated to explaining how our compensation program works. Our prospect will have three questions concerning this area:

How much will it cost me?

What do I have to do?

How much can I make?

By answering, "How much will it cost me?" right away, it will put our prospect at ease. Most "salesmen" will wait to the very end to spring the price on a prospect. We will do just the opposite. We don't want our prospect thinking throughout our presentation, "How much is this going to cost me?"

"What do I have to do?" has already been answered in the training section. Just set a few appointments and watch us build your group!

"How much can I make?" is easy. We just give a quick overview of our marketing plan and maybe a couple of examples of what others have done in the business.

That's all there is to a great, professional presentation. No mystery at all. If we just answer our prospect's five basic questions, we will sponsor with ease. And the best part is that is usually takes less than 25 or 30 minutes!

And don't worry about the close. When we are done, all we have to do is just ask him if this is for him or not. There is really very little reason to think it over. All the questions have been answered. No need for high pressure.

Distributor Joe took careful notes and planned to attend another competitor's network marketing meeting the following week. It was cheap entertainment and Distributor Joe always enjoyed a good laugh.

Food For Thought

*"Thoughts determine
what you want . . .
Action determines
what you get."*

Think about it.

—Big Al

Want to sponsor more distributors? Want to sponsor better distributors? Want to build an incredible large and stable MLM organization?

Big Al's MLM Sponsoring Secrets album contains the very best recruiting techniques for you and your downline. The information is awesome and easy to use.

Get eight CDs with Big Al's best recruiting secrets. Plus, you get <u>four additional</u> CDs with his basic training workshop, *Big Al Live in London* — free. The entire set of 12 audio training CDs can be ordered by contacting:

Here are <u>four</u> <u>more</u> *Big Al Recruiting Books* you'll want in your library:

#2 How To Create A Recruiting Explosion. This book contains more advanced recruiting techniques such as:

- ◆ Locating the fishing hole for the best prospects
- ◆ Too good to be true
- ◆ The checklist close - the easy way to decide
- ◆ Trade show challenges and rewards
- ◆ Finding the best people
- ◆ Ad techniques that work independently
- ◆ Handling questions
- ◆ Street smarts
- ◆ Solving office problems
- ◆ And the all-time blockbuster recruiting technique, *The Stair Step Solution!* This is the way to build 20 to 30 new distributors *F-A-S-T!*

#3 Turbo MLM. Accelerate your group-building with this third book in the *Big Al* Recruiting Series. Turbo-charge your recruiting methods by using:

- ◆ The million dollar close
- ◆ Mail order recruiting
- ◆ Handling money handicaps
- ◆ Sorting for true leaders
- ◆ Tale of two winners
- ◆ Dangers of over training
- ◆ Why prospects don't join
- ◆ And, the all-time super income builder: *The Presentation Ratings Game.*

#4 *How To Build MLM Leaders For Fun & Profit.* Build massive downline organizations by building independent motivated leaders. Your group is only as strong as its leaders. Special sections on:

- ◆ Cloning superhuman leaders
- ◆ The $93,000 Recruiting System
- ◆ Piggy-back your opportunity
- ◆ Ninja mail
- ◆ The file drawer method
- ◆ Hype from the top
- ◆ The 2% myth
- ◆ How to get all the prospects you want
- ◆ Streamlining your business for extra profit
- ◆ Man Kills Family Pet principle
- ◆ And much, much more

Just pick from the many easy methods and systems to build your leader network fast.

#5 *Super Prospecting: Special Offers & Quick-Start Systems.* Put your new distributor to work in less than three minutes with the A.S.K. recruiting system, starting on page 77. This no-wait system makes recruiting easy for shy, busy, or brand new distributors. Special sections on:

- ◆ How to turn ordinary people into eager prospects
- ◆ The introvert's way to getting opportunity presentations
- ◆ The secret word in great offers
- ◆ What if your entire recruiting promotional budget was only $600?
- ◆ Guidelines for your personal audiocassette tape
- ◆ Sample script for your audiocassette tape
- ◆ And much, much more

Make your offers irresistible, get prospects to come to you. It maybe the best *Big Al* book ever published!

Volume Discounts

All *Big Al* Recruiting Books are $12.95 each.

For the professional leader who wishes to take advantage of *Big Al's* surprisingly generous quantity discounts, please contact:

KAAS Publishing
P.O. Box 890084
Houston, TX 77289 USA

http://www.fortunenow.com

Visa, MasterCard, Discover and American Express orders
Phone (281) 280-9800

Feel a bit shy when approaching strangers? Would you like to turn acquaintances into hot, eager prospects? How can you approach potential prospects about your business without looking like a greedy salesman searching for a quick commission?

How To Get Rich Without Winning The Lottery, by Keith Schreiter is easy to read, easy to implement, and shows how anyone, a carpenter, a rocket scientist, a housewife, or even a lawyer (gasp!) can follow the simple principles to accumulate wealth. And the best part is that this book will show your prospects how to add network marketing to their wealth plan if they wish.

This is a gift that will build a long-term relationship. So leave a copy of this book with that cab driver who gave you good service, to that hotel employee who helped you set up your opportunity meeting, to the waitress with the million-dollar smile, and to your best friend who would like to be rich, but doesn't knew how.

Once you read this book, your life will never be the same. You'll be on the direct road to financial independence even without the help of network marketing. And because you already do network marketing, you'll be way ahead on this million-dollar road to riches. The book is so good, you won't want to give away your personal copy.

Give the books away?

Yes. These books were meant to given away as gifts that will instantly bond you with your prospect.

And the price? A little more than $1 each in quantities. About the cost of an audiocassette tape, but so much more impressive.

The proof is in the results. First, you'll personally love the book as it will quickly direct you to the most direct road to wealth. Second, you'll love the instant relationships this book creates with your prospects. Now you have something really important to talk about. And third, the book pre-sells network marketing so that your prospect is ready to take advantage of your business opportunity.

To order, contact:

KAAS Publishing
P.O. Box 890084
Houston, TX 77289 USA

http://www.fortunenow.com

Visa, MasterCard, Discover and American Express orders
Phone (281) 280-9800

How To Give A
One-Minute
Presentation

By Tom Schreiter

Learn how to get a presentation appointment with 100% of the prospects you talk to, and give your prospects a COMPLETE presentation in only one minute!

Stop doing network marketing the hard way.

Learn the two sentences that will get your prospects to literally beg you for an instant presentation.

Learn how to give a complete, total, beginning-to-end presentation in only one minute!

And watch your prospects' eyes light up when they see how easy it is.

To order this 3-CD audio album, contact:

KAAS Publishing
P.O. Box 890084
Houston, TX 77289 USA

http://www.fortunenow.com

Visa, MasterCard, Discover and American Express orders
Phone (281) 280-9800